HOW TO DEAL WITH DIFFICULT PEOPLE

Master Effective Communication Skills So You Can Deal With Difficult People

(Learn How to Deal With a Difficult Person)

Latonya Hook

Published by Sharon Lohan

© **Latonya Hook**

All Rights Reserved

How to Deal With Difficult People: Master Effective Communication Skills So You Can Deal With Difficult People (Learn How to Deal With a Difficult Person)

ISBN 978-1-990334-75-7

All rights reserved. No part of this guide may be reproduced in any form without permission in writing from the publisher except in the case of brief quotations embodied in critical articles or reviews.

Legal & Disclaimer

The information contained in this book is not designed to replace or take the place of any form of medicine or professional medical advice. The information in this book has been provided for educational and entertainment purposes only.

The information contained in this book has been compiled from sources deemed reliable, and it is accurate to the best of the Author's knowledge; however, the Author cannot guarantee its accuracy and validity and cannot be held liable for any errors or omissions. Changes are periodically made to this book. You must consult your doctor or get professional medical advice before using any of the suggested remedies, techniques, or information in this book.

Upon using the information contained in this book, you agree to hold harmless the Author from and against any damages, costs, and expenses, including any legal fees potentially resulting from the application of any of the information provided by this guide. This disclaimer applies to any damages or injury caused by the use and application, whether directly or indirectly, of any advice or information presented, whether for breach of contract, tort, negligence, personal injury, criminal intent, or under any other cause of action.

You agree to accept all risks of using the information presented inside this book. You need to consult a professional medical practitioner in order to ensure you are both able and healthy enough to participate in this program.

Table of Contents

INTRODUCTION 1

CHAPTER 1: MORE FORCEFUL STRATEGIES FOR DEALING WITH DIFFICULT PEOPLE AT WORK 3

CHAPTER 2: DIFFERENT TYPES OF DIFFICULT PEOPLE 12

CHAPTER 3: THE GOSSIP 24

CHAPTER 4: STRATEGIES TO MANAGE DIFFICULT BEHAVIOR 32

CHAPTER 5: HOW TO MOTIVATE YOUR WORKERS 39

CHAPTER 6: INTERACTING WITH DIFFICULT PEOPLE 55

CHAPTER 7: WILL POWER TO DEAL WITH DIFFICULT PEOPLE 63

CHAPTER 8: CHANGING YOUR ENVIRONMENT 88

CHAPTER 9: GOSSIPING EMPLOYEES 118

CONCLUSION 131

Introduction

Most of us come across difficult people in our lives. We may have to deal with an irrational individual at work or within the household. It can be quite easy to allow others to affect us and ruin our day, but what type of actions can we take to avoid these situations? The first step is to empower yourself so that you can be aware of the different perspectives that may help you to counter these forces. This book contains proven steps and strategies on how to deal with the four main types of difficult people: the bossy, the negative, the needy, and the tactless. Each one requires a different approach to handle them accordingly.

The tips and lessons you can find here will teach you how to properly interact, converse, and stand firm on your personality and beliefs without having to trample a difficult person or end your relationship with them. You will also learn how to gradually change them for the better without them realizing it.

So, not only can empowering yourself on how deal with these type of personalities be beneficial for you, but you may also aid to improve the lives of others by helping them to reach their full potential (even if this is not your intent). In my conclusion, I will also share with you the greatest lesson that I learned about difficult people and how that important lesson permanently changed my life for the better!

Thanks again for downloading this book. I hope you enjoy it!

Chapter 1: More Forceful Strategies For Dealing With Difficult People At Work

Now you've done your part in attempting a non-confrontational approach. Unfortunately, your difficult coworker is still getting in your hair. It's time to gather up your courage and take a more active approach.

☐ Speak with the person whom you are having a problem with.

Engage them in a private discussion. Make sure that you begin your speech with an "I" statement instead of a "You" statement. "You" statements tend to sound accusatory and the person may feel like you are attacking him.

Example: Begin with: "I feel like there's been a bit of misunderstanding between you and me."

Don't blurt out: "You said some really nasty stuff about me to others."

Try to convey your message clearly. Explain to your colleague the impact of his behavior on you. Meanwhile, maintain a pleasant atmosphere. It's possible that they don't have any idea at all of how their actions are affecting you.

What could possibly go wrong? Well, the worst case would be that the person may know all along how they're affecting you and they may try to deny it or they might make an attempt to explain their way out of it. Sadly, there are simply those who just don't give a damn as in the case of individuals suffering from antisocial personality disorder. Whatever you do, make sure that the discussion is productive. That is, try to come up with an agreement about positive actions that will enable you both to move forward.

☐Follow up after the first discussion.

Sometime after the initial conversation, determine whether your colleague's behavior has improved, or perhaps, did it get worse? Then, decide on whether a follow-up talk is required. Ask yourself: If I speak with him again, will it help? Then, decide on whether you wish to pursue the matter by yourself. Is it time to bring other people into the picture? Do you think your boss will support you in case you decide to escalate the problem? That said, try to maintain peace for as long as possible.

☐ Have a public confrontation.

This doesn't have to be as bad as it sounds. You may handle your coworker's negative behavior through gentle humor or mild sarcasm. Sometimes, overstated physical gestures might work as a response. Nope, you're not being advised to give your colleague the finger. These physical gestures could be in the form of a salute or placing your hand over your chest to express an exaggerated sense of feeling hurt. Unfortunately, not everyone is capable of pulling off these positive confrontational strategies. If this simply isn't your style, then move on to the next step.

☐ Get others involved.

As previously mentioned, you should only involve people who are affected by the problem or have the capacity to solve the problem. If you're convinced that you've done everything that you could've possibly done, then it's time to have a talk with your boss or your HR representative. The moment you do this, be aware that you are escalating the issue. When you speak with your boss, make sure that you present the matter not as an interpersonal conflict but as an issue that has a serious effect on your work. Be clear as to what the difficult coworker is doing or saying.

☐ Gather other affected co-workers.

If more than one person approaches the management regarding the same issue, then the chances of being heard increases. It might need a group of people in order to convince your manager that the effect of the difficult person's behavior is actually more extensive and more serious than it seems. However, you should do this carefully. When handled poorly, it may look like you've just gathered a bunch of workmates to gang up on one employee.

☐ If these approaches don't work...

Then it may be time to get back to non-confrontational approaches. Limit the difficult co-worker's access to you. Work with projects that have nothing to do with that employee. Simply put, avoid your difficult coworker but don't let that avoidance cripple your career growth. Alternatively, you may opt to transfer to a new position within the organization.

How to Handle a Confrontation

The thing about not being able to confront a difficult colleague is that you end up having make-believe confrontations in your head. Perhaps you lie at bed awake at night playing out conversations with the fellow worker that you are angry with. The problem here is that you're not only allowing the difficult coworker to affect your work life but your personal life as well. The stress brought about by these mental conversations can have a negative impact on your health and your personal relationships. When a difficult coworker is causing you to toss and turn in bed at night, then it might be time to have that real confrontation.

☐ Begin by stating the problem in a single (or a couple of) non-emotional statements that are based on facts.

For instance, if you want to confront a partner for taking all of the credit for a project that the two of you accomplished together, do not start by saying: "Hey, you stole all the credit for the Waverly account!" Instead, say something like: "It looked like I had no part in the Waverly account. My name did not even appear on the document."

Notice that while this approach started with an "I" statement, it isn't an "I feel" statement and thus, it cannot be dismissed as an emotional statement. Remember that stating facts are important. That way, the difficult colleague will have a hard time disputing your statement.

☐ Say your initial statement and then stop.

While it might feel tempting to keep talking and release all of your frustrations in one go, you should restrain yourself and allow the difficult coworker to respond. You may have this instant urge to justify your initial statement with a supporting statement, but there is really no sense in defending yourself. You may also feel like you already know how the other person is going to answer, hence, increasing your impulse to speak further. However, remember that this confrontation is to achieve a solution, not so you can vent your frustrations. So just state the non-emotional, fact-based problem and then wait for your fellow worker to reply.

☐ Avoid arguing.

As said earlier, confrontations don't necessarily have to end up in a nasty fight. In fact, this discussion is meant to be productive. Listen to what your workfellow has to say. Sometimes, there really is no need to blame anyone for anything. Sometimes, it really isn't necessary to prove who's right and who's wrong.

☐ Concentrate on the real issue.

Prior to the confrontation, determine the conflict resolution that you desire. The kind of conflict resolution that you want will enable you to define how you are going to initiate the confrontation and in what direction you are going to stir the conversation. There are only two ways this will go down—either the person will agree with you or not. When you confront the co-worker using an accusatory approach, his response will naturally turn out to be defensive. At this point, it is necessary to avoid getting into an argument and elaborating. Stick to the real issue. Your coworker can easily worm his way out of the current subject by directing the conversation to another direction. So do not get sidetracked by other concerns that might be unearthed during the process. In the end, remember that you are looking to negotiate and not to pick a fight.

Chapter 2: Different Types Of Difficult People

There are many different types of difficult people that you may run into during your life. Understanding these people can help you understand how to deal with these people in the best way. Understanding the fundamentals of what makes difficult people act the way that they do can help you find ways to work around the difficulties that these people pose for you.

When Difficult People are Your Fault

You first must understand the fact that what you need or want is not the same as what others need or want. When you experience conflict between your goals and someone else's, you may perceive the other person as being difficult. In reality, he or she is not necessarily a difficult person.

It is important to become more empathetic and patient. Just because someone does not want the same things that you do does not mean that he or she is a bad person. Sometimes, it is really you being difficult because you refuse to bend. Understanding when you are being difficult is important. You can determine when you are hurting others and you can change your behavior so that you are more flexible.

Flexibility is crucial when you are trying to work with other people. You are not the only person in the universe. While you are entitled to your own preferences and desires, you are not entitled to always getting your way with other people. Sometimes, you have to accept the fact that what you want is not best for everyone involved. When you are working with other people, sometimes a compromise or other arrangement is necessary.

When it seems that everyone in your life is difficult, you may want to reevaluate the situation. Is everyone being difficult? Or are you being hard-headed? You are probably the common denominator when everyone seems to be working against you. It is time for you to make some sort of change.

Stop blaming other people for being difficult all of the time. Start to consider that you need to bend and be a little flexible. Things cannot always go exactly your way. Accept that other people have different needs and desires than you and will fight you for things that go against their beliefs or needs.

Communication is key in this situation. You should clearly communicate what you need. Then find out what other people need. Make people feel needed and valued by listening to them and focusing on their input. Once you do that, you have the grounds to begin making progress with the "difficult people" in your life. Whether that progress involves reaching a mutual solution or compromising, you can achieve it when you facilitate decent communication.

Dramatic

There are certain people in your life who will prefer pitching a fit than just working with you toward a goal. These people lower the quality of your life by adding drama and stress to it. You cannot seem to work with such people. You even come to fear them and hate them because of the stress and turmoil that they cause.

It is important to understand that dramatic people are running a form of manipulation on you. Much like small children pitching violent temper tantrums over candy in the middle of the grocery store, these people have learned that overreacting will get them what they want. They are used to bulldozing their way through people's barriers by acting like babies. If you take a close look at how dramatic people act, you will find many similarities with babies, actually.

Dramatic people will be difficult to you in many ways. They will overreact to everything. They will spread rumors about you and start fights with you. They will steal the spotlight from you all the time. No matter what they do, they will lower the quality of your life with their dramatic antics.

Rude

Rude people are great at just ruining your day. By being rude to you, they let you know that your feelings have no relevance to them. They make you feel worthless and less than human. You often wish you could just be rude to these people right back, but often you cannot, especially if you are encountering these rude people at work. Customer service is an example of a job where you must fake a smile and tolerate rudeness. Dealing with family sometimes calls for you to endure the rudeness of overbearing family members, who don't care when you confront them.

The most important thing is to be empathetic and to not take things personally. Rude people are usually rude because of their own issues, not because they hate you. Try to be understanding and you will find that the rudeness hurts a little less. You can also try being rude right back and setting up boundaries with these types of difficult people.

Stubborn

A stubborn person poses the ultimate hitch in all of your plans. Stubborn people refuse to give you a break or let you have any leeway. You must do what they want and you stand no chance to get your way.

A mixture of flexibility, teamwork, and persuasion can do wonders in making stubborn people budge. You want to be empathetic and you want to work with a stubborn person toward some sort of mutual goal. You also want to convince a stubborn person to give up his or her ego in favor of what you want. You can only accomplish this by using persuasion and great communication. Cultivate a sense of teamwork.

Uncertain

These are the people who drive you crazy with their uncertainty. These are "maybe people," who never have a clear yes or no answer. Their fickleness and unsureness make them difficult to be around and difficult to work with. You want to scream, "Make up your damn mind!" but you can't. If you work in sales or on teams, you probably deal with people like this all of the time. While it is infuriating, you cannot rush or pressure an uncertain person.

Instead, you can use persuasion to sway and convince uncertain people. You can also offer negative consequences to fickle people so that they will stop changing their minds on you. Be fickle right back or cut a fickle person out of your life to stop flaky behavior.

Insecure

Everyone has some type of insecurity. Insecurities are a natural facet of human nature. Humans often find comfort in locating their own faults because the human brain is programmed to focus more on the negative than the positive. But excessively insecure people can be very difficult because they do not believe in themselves at all. They are riddled with trust issues and they say terrible things about themselves. You may find it hurtful to see how much these insecure people suffer. Or you may just think that they are annoying and looking for attention.

Whatever reason that an insecure person proves to be difficult for you to contend with, you have to use some empathy and try not to take his or her insecurities personally. He or she probably suffers a great deal and does not mean to be so annoying. In addition, he or she probably needs some tenderness and love. If you simply cannot stand being around an insecure person, then consider cutting ties or offering tough love to teach the insecure person to be stronger. You do not have to enable insecure behavior by offering a person comfort and compliments all of the time. An insecure person who is starving for attention will quickly snap out of it if you react with tough love. Just be careful not to break a truly insecure person's heart by being too tough.

People who are Never Happy

We all know that one whiny, pessimistic person. This person always whines and complains, to the point where it appears he or she just loves being miserable. He or she asks us for advice but disregards it in order to stay unhappy. There are ways this person could fix his or her problems, but he or she staunchly refuses to do anything.

Understand that this person is just in a negative place. It is not your duty to console, comfort, or advise this negative person. Just put distance or tune out his or her negative words. Stay positive. You do not need such bad forces in your life.

Sneaky and Underhanded

Sneaky people are hard to deal with. This is because you do not know what their real intentions are or what they are really doing. They do things you do not want without your knowledge. They work to undermine your authority, as well.

This sneakiness is not nice. It can be very frustrating. It can also make you question your relationship with this person, as he or she has proved to not be trustworthy. How can you manage such a person? The answer is complex. You must use a combination of deflection, persuasion, and negative consequences to make such people respect your boundaries.

People You Love

This may seem like a joke. But think about it. Probably the people who pose the biggest challenges in your life are the people whom you love the most. Your love and the fact that you spend a lot of time around these people make them so difficult. You constantly worry about your family and friends, and you fight for them. You are annoyed by their personality flaws and quirks but you also love them. Loved ones can be the most difficult because they know that they can get away with it.

Good communication can help you resolve almost all differences with loved ones.

Your loved ones are likely to lie, fight, and rebel to keep their own freedom. Try not to be over controlling. Instead, be understanding.

Chapter 3: The Gossip

Gossips abound in organizations with poor management style or those with a lot of organizational issues. When not properly handled, gossips can bring serious problems in the workplace. Gossips can weaken employee morale and ultimately result in inefficiencies and lower productivity. Here are some ways you can deal with people who love to spread gossip in the workplace.

Make sure that you set a good example

This is particularly true for managers and supervisors who wish to lessen or eradicate gossip in the workplace. You need to make sure that you do not spread gossip in order to stop other people from saying that they are only following your steps. Do not gossip about your other colleagues, especially your boss. Do not make idle speculations. Do not complain about company policies in front of your colleagues. If you like doing these things, do not be surprised when the people under you are doing exactly what you are doing. When you set a good example, your subordinates will have someone to look up to and follow.

Openly receive issues and concerns

When your colleagues sense that you are not willing to listen to them when it comes to problems and issues in the workplace, they may resort to spreading gossip just to voice their thoughts out. If they think that they cannot talk to you directly, to will just share their complaints with one another. If they sense that you are not willing to give them clear answers to their concerns and queries, they will just end up speculating among themselves.

Make sure that your communication lines are always open

You should not only willingly listen to the concerns and issues of your colleagues and subordinates but you should also make sure that you appropriately disclose information that your team and subordinates need to hear. Do not make them seek information from other people. When there are issues to be resolved, it is better that you be open to your team so you can cooperate and work towards the resolution. Transparency in your team will enable you to gain the trust and support of your team which can ultimately lessen gossips and speculations.

Do not shoot the messenger

Many gossips start when someone "shoots the messenger". Do not take negative actions such as reprimanding people who courageously raise issues to you. When you do so, they will no longer have the initiative to openly discuss issues with you. Your colleagues and subordinates may simply opt to complain and speculate amongst themselves than to bear the brunt.

Learn how to confront people who love to spread gossips

When rumormongers are allowed to spread their gossips without any negative consequences, they will think that it is alright to do so. On the other hand, if you let a rumormonger know that you are well aware of the gossips he has been spreading about you, the rumormonger will likelystop spreading the gossip. He may even be compelled to stop gossiping when he learns that his gossips can actually hurt other people's feelings. When you confront a person about the gossips that they spread, you will not only stop that person from spreading more gossips but you will also stop other people from joining in spreading the gossips.

Learn how to deal with the problem and not with the person spreading the gossip

When you finally decide to confront a gossipmonger, it is advisable that you concentrate on the issue being talked about and onthe other person's behaviors instead of on the person. You will definitely look more professional when you do so. Instead of saying"You are evil for spreading gossips about me", you can opt to simply say"I'm getting concerned about the gossips that you are spreadingand I want you to stop doing it." When you react this way, you will not appear as a hostile person to other people who might be listening to your conversation.

Do not allow yourself to be sucked in by the situation

One of the best ways to stop rumors and gossips in the workplace is to refuse being sucked in. When someone urges you to give a comment about a person who is not present, you can decline and simply change the subject in a subtle manner. When you do so, the gossip will not continue to grow and people will have other better things to talk about.

Verify gossips by asking questions

There are times when you cannot really avoid being in the middle of a gossip and you cannot simply change the topic to other matters. When you this happens to you, you can just validate the information that they are talking about. Ask questions about the exact time, place and other specific details. Most likely, people do not realize that they only know basic information about the subject being discussed. When you ask for the specific details, you are basically forcing the issue in a subtle manner since anyone who cannot give specific information basically acknowledges the lack of credibility of the gossip being spread. When gossipmongers cannot give you the specific details, you can simply reply back "I think all that information is quite vague. Do you really think it can be true?" By saying this, you are clearly telling the gossips that you are having doubts about the things that they are telling you.

Focus on coming up with solutions

A lot of gossips arise when workers or employees are concerned about a certain issue. When you hear people starting to complain or gossip, remind yourself of that old saying "It is better to light a single candle than to curse the darkness." Rather than adding to the complaints, you can encourage others to start thinking about possible solutions. You should not expect that you will always come up with solutions that management will readily accept. Still, the practice of concentrating on solutions will prevent people from spreading gossips.

Avoid being self-righteous

When doing any of the techniques discussed above, you need to avoid doing them in a self-righteous manner. Do not brag about your efforts to stop gossips. And you should definitely avoid becoming haughty and start lecturing your colleagues how gossiping is bad. When you become self-righteous, you will just be alienating your colleagues. You simply have to be casual about how you deal with gossips so you will not create new problems that you need to deal with.

Chapter 4: Strategies To Manage Difficult Behavior

In this chapter we shall explore different strategies on how to deal with difficult people and get the best from them. Since we can't run away from them, we have to find a way of interacting with them in the best possible way to reduce frustrations on our part. Just as we had seen earlier, people are not normally difficult but under certain circumstances, they might exhibit difficult behavior. We should know of how to deal with this kind of behavior and also tell what situations lead to them and how to avoid them if we can.

The overriding reason people become difficult is due to some form of insecurity or inadequacy. Lack of self-esteem, or social skills might also lead to difficult behavior. A small percentage of people are just aggressive in nature. They will be mean and loud in all situations. However, most difficult people are passive aggressors. They may appear very pleasant and will offer niceties at any opportunity but will also engage in some negative behaviors.

The first strategy when dealing with difficult people is to never take their behavior personally. No matter what they try to do, do not take any offence and focus more on finding a solution rather than dwelling on what they did. Managing our emotions and expectation of people go a long way in reducing frustrations when we encounter aggressive and difficult behavior. When you are dealing with a difficult person never reduce it to personal attacks. Don't become defensive as this might be what their plan is. Stick to the issues at hand and the facts along. Also remember it's not about winning rather than working out how best to relate to each other.

The second strategy is to realize that you can never change someone. This is very critical as some people think that it's possible for a colleague or a partner to change. People never change, they can just pretend for a short time. So the only solution is to understand their behavior and developing strategies to deal with it. The only way a person can change their behavior is through their own personal initiative and this will take some time too. Many managers at work spend a lot of time trying to change an employee to be what they want only to get frustrated when they do not do it. If anybody has to change, then it will only be you. You will need to change your emotional and behavioral responses to difficult personalities. This is by equipping yourself with skills to deal with them.

Dealing with aggressive people

When it comes to aggressive people who might get hostile in their interactions, you'll require to be absolutely clear with them that you do not tolerate their behavior and you will report them to the authorities if they attempt to do something violent. You should interact with them at a neutral place and probably have a third party to keep them in check. If you correspond with them through electronic means, keep a record of the interaction for any future reference. Remember you should never feel threatened somebody's actions. Also don't be angry or otherwise because if so, the other person will have control over you. If you really feel overwhelmed, you'd rather excuse yourself and take some time to regain composure.

Do not judge

It's very tempting to pass judgment on someone based on their behavior. We are quick to label people with some unpleasant names. The bad thing with this is that the person might have been going through a hard time with life's pressures and just reacted in a way that doesn't reflect their true character. Unfortunately, once we label somebody, we will forever view them as that label.

Establish facts

When you encounter a situation, aim first to establish all the facts before you offer a solution. Fast actions are needed from all in today's world, but first establish the facts. Don't allow emotions get in the way of your decision making. You might tend to get angry with a person since they didn't react the way you envisioned, but this shouldn't lead you to making an emotionally charged decision. You might only regret it later. Don't yell or get overly animated. You might be getting worked up on the inside but you must master your self-control. Communication can be through nonverbal means as well, so master your body's language and don't let it give away your emotions. If you allow emotions to get in the way, your team will see you as not being objective. When dealing with difficult people, this would be the last thing you want.

Wait before you react.

When faced with some difficult situations created by a colleague or friend, we tend to react fast in a way that we only regret later. The heat of the moment overcomes us and we say things we shouldn't have said. Whether it's through word of mouth or written communication, we should take some time to let things cool off and approach them with a sober head. At times we don't even need to respond at all. Never lower yourself to mediocrity levels by allowing yourself to respond to negativity. When you fail to respond, you completely disarm the difficult person and alters their pre meditated course of action.

Remove negative people from your life

In certain situations you should remove certain people from your life. Overly negative people who never see anything good will only end up draining you emotionally and inflicting you with their negativity. It will be in your own best interests if you go rid of them. However, if it is not be possible to remove them, for example, if they are colleagues at work or at school and for one reason or another you must work with them, reduce your interactions to the bare necessity. With this, they'll understand your boundaries and will not interfere with them.

Chapter 5: How To Motivate Your Workers

One management duty that novice and experienced managers alike sometimes struggle with is the motivation of staff. It's easy to think that the only things people care about are money and job title – something concrete that they can point to – but the good news for those of us with lower paid workers, is that it isn't always the case.

There are widely thought to be two kinds of motivation:

Extrinsic motivation: This is when the employee is motivated by something outside of him or herself, such as financial reward (pay) or job title. They may have no interest in a specific job at hand but if it will bring them an external reward – good grades, a pay rise or a new job title – they will do it anyway. They work for exterior rewards rather than for the fun of it. They are focused on the reward and not the action. The problem here, of course, is that it's just not possible to reward people each and every time they do something; that's when someone only driven by extrinsic motivation becomes demotivated.

Intrinsic motivation: In contrast, intrinsic motivation comes from within the employee; it is when an employee does something just for the fun of it, because they like to learn something new or because they think it is the right thing to do. Intrinsic motivation is usually stronger than extrinsic motivation and doesn't rely on other people. For these employees, a job well done is satisfaction enough. Often congratulating these people is reward itself. To encourage these employees, you should ideally pay them a fair wage and then take money out of the equation after that; don't even mention it as a factor. They probably won't. If you can make these employees believe in your values and be happy to work towards them, you have a powerful motivational tool. You can encourage intrinsic motivation by praising when praise is due, offering potential for extra responsibility and encouraging initiative. Allow a degree of freedom in their work for the employee to identify their own intrinsic motivation. And listen! Listen when they tell you what drives them or pay attention when they seem enthused by a task; once you understand the factors that motivate them, you can appeal to it again and again.

Each employee will be driven by a slightly different mix of these two motivators; some will be primarily extrinsic while others will be intrinsic, while another segment of your workforce entirely will need a healthy mix of both. Your challenge as a manager will be to identify who needs what in order to be enthused at work. The more you can encourage intrinsic motivation, the longer your staff will probably stay motivated.

You could say, therefore, that the key to having highly motivated staff is to recruit people who naturally love what they do and want to do it for its own sake and not for any external reward; if they are good at it, they earn the internal affirmation of a job well done.

Here's a question for you: Should you expect your staff to be self-motivated? I'm going to say yes... in a way. You see, the harsh fact of the matter is that you cannot actually motivate your staff; it may come as a surprise, but no matter what you do, you cannot make them feel motivation if they don't. You can't make them want to work extra hours to get that order out, even if you do offer extra money for it. Neither can you encourage them to step up with the promise of recognition, career advancement or a new role if they don't care about it in the first place. You cannot make them feel motivated and happy in their role; they have to do that themselves. What you can do, however, is to create the right sort of environment in which motivation can thrive. If someone is motivated by recognition, make sure good work is praised; if someone else is motivated by the thought of stepping up to take more responsibility, make sure career advancement is prized and achievable.

Don't fall into the trap of thinking basic manual work or low paid jobs have to lack motivation either; they don't. It may not set the world on fire to flip burgers in a fast-food restaurant but sometimes the reward of an honest day's work can be enough to motivate. So too can a pleasant working environment where the employee can actually enjoy their day.

Don't assume that you can't motivate these people just because they are in low paid jobs; it may sometimes seem like an uphill struggle but at the end of the day there is nothing more demotivating than a boss who doesn't expect more from his or her team. A boss who expects staff morale to be low or for employees not to want more from their jobs is one who is perpetuating negativity. Take the time to find out what does motivate every single member of your team, from the bottom to the top, and make sure you can provide it.

Try to find motivators other than money; there's never enough money to go around and an employee who only works for a wage packet is never going to be loyal. In fact, let me tell you something: recent studies have found that in many cases offering extrinsic or external financial rewards for employees to complete a task has actually made the task less interesting for them. Extrinsic rewards have reduced intrinsic motivation. This doesn't happen in every case, of course, and it's certainly not a reason to avoid paying a fair wage, but some employees will take more pleasure from completing a task because they find it interesting than they will if you pay them to do it. So never assume that a lower paid worker is only in it for the money; they very well might be BUT you may just not have tapped into their intrinsic motivation yet. That's your next task.

The more hospitable you can make the work environment, the better motivation will thrive. Even the most self-motivated of individuals will start to become disheartened if his efforts at improvement are constantly thwarted or not recognised.

The Importance of Motivation

Why is motivation so important? Why can't you just rely on people to do as they are told without needing incentive? Well, people might... for a little while. But once a team loses morale, their work and working environment begin to suffer. People may start taking more sick days, their productivity falls and customer service deteriorates. Indeed, absenteeism costs UK industry £11.5bn annually. Likewise, a high staff turnover, which runs at 125% in some industries, involves huge recruiting costs and money spent on overtime as other people have to make up the shortfall. And don't forget word of mouth; if staff are unhappy, they are not likely to recommend your company to anyone. Indeed, they may even run it down.

Needless to say, you can't afford to ignore morale.

So, what can you do to Motivate People?

Here are some suggestions:

Recognise their contributions; take the time to notice the effort they're putting in. It may feel strange or awkward for you to formally or publicly praise someone in the beginning – it's often not a skill new or middle managers are taught — but once you see the pleasure that recognition brings, you'll understand just how powerful it can be. Remember, praise in public, reprimand in private.

Reward them with praise and not with financial bonuses unless the bonus is tied into something specific such as targets set ahead of time, project work, an annual bonus scheme or a one-off bonus to recognise their hard work. Never use a bonus as a bribe to take on new work unless it's tied into targets. The danger with bonuses is that they set a potential precedent and employees will come to expect, want or demand a bonus for every new piece of work you want them to take on. A bonus should be a reward for good work after the fact and not a sweetener to do work that needs to be done. See our section on employees who ask for a pay rise in the second part of this book to see how you can handle staff members who ask for financial rewards. A good reward is giving someone a greater freedom to use their own initiative and creativity within the workplace. If an employee consistently shows impressive work, you might want to reward them with more responsibility or a leadership role. Most people are inspired by leadership roles, so be creative. Even informal leadership positions can boost morale; appoint a member of staff to greet visitors and show them around, for instance, or to go into schools and talk about what your company does. The boost in morale won't just be restricted to the employee taking on the new role either; it will benefit the whole team to see that hard work and results are appreciated and rewarded.

Mentor, mentor, mentor: Re-read the mentoring section of this book; it's a huge bonus to morale. Don't forget; you can appoint one of your experienced staff to mentor others; it's as great way to show trust and place them in a position of leadership.

Make sure they have the training they need: Keep the training door open; people are much more responsive if they feel the company is taking the time to invest in them. There is no such thing as too much training, so keep offering 'top-up' training courses. These don't have to be done off-site or by external companies; in some cases, it may be as simple as holding refreshers to make sure everyone is up to date with the latest health and safety rules or the latest skills. Take advantage of members of your team who show particular aptitude at certain tasks; let them teach others. It's a great morale-booster for both sides.

Job titles: Some managers are very reluctant to offer changes in job titles, but it can actually be a great morale booster if there's no money left in the kitty. Just make it clear that the change in job title does not come with a new salary. Be as creative with titles as you like; you want to show appreciation for your employee and allow them to boost their self-esteem. If they are happy to announce their job title at dinner parties, for instance, you have cracked it. You can even allow individual staff members to have input into their own job title (of course, it doesn't mean that you have to take their suggestion if there's a legitimate reason not to do so, but a compromise could keep both sides happy).

Career development: Employees tend to get a little demotivated if they can't see room for growth in the company; there's nothing worse than a dead-end job to make people question why they even get out of bed in the morning. Work with them to develop their potential career path in the company; give them something to aim for. Promoting people from within

– while not always possible, granted – is certainly laudable and sends a very positive message.

Make sure you have a positive working environment. This applies to the actual environment and machines, technology or the space around you as much as to the leadership from the top. Never play the blame game, for instance, or rule by terror if you want a happy workforce. The latter may seem to get work done but it isn't sustainable over the long haul. Get ready for a steady turnover of staff if that's your preferred management style.

Chocolate day! It may sound flippant but introducing special days or lunches can give a much needed break from routine. It could be as simple as chocolate day every Wednesday (where you buy a chocolate bar for each member of your team) or a weekly or monthly pizza lunch (where you again buy the pizza for the team – and allow them the time to sit and enjoy it!) Fit it around your team's working day and announce it in advance; it may sound like a small gesture, but people will get excited about it. I once worked in a company where the bosses held 'State of the Nation' meetings once a month. In these meetings, we'd learn the latest figures and news from across the company, someone would be singled out for praise (Employee of the Month) and, even better, there was a company-sponsored bonding session in the pub afterwards! Those meetings, while not compulsory, were always very well attended!

Don't think that just because you're not the CEO of the company, you're not responsible for morale. You are. Line managers actually have a bigger part to play in the motivation of their staff than they realise.

Dilys Robinson of the Institute for Employment Studies says: "It is often the line manager who is predominantly responsible for the mood of the team, and an effective, encouraging, engaging manager can motivate the team to produce excellent results even when times are difficult."

Never underestimate how your own mood and behaviour can impact on your team, as indeed can your personality. You are the manager; it's fair to say that you set the tone for your environment. Your employees look to you for guidance. If you're sad, angry, agitated or in a bad mood, that's going to trickle down through every single member of your team. You will put a damper on morale just by being there. Staff may choose to keep their heads down to avoid confrontation or even become paranoid, thinking your bad mood is because of them. They are going to be less likely to raise their head above the parapet and suggest new ideas or raise issues; your moodiness therefore may directly contribute to a lack of creativity, a potential death knell for any business. Avoid it by working hard to keep your emotions on an even keel.

So get your thinking cap on and be prepared to make re-affirming gestures, big and small, as part of your normal day. Your staff will certainly thank you for it.

Chapter 6: Interacting With Difficult People

The best thing in the world is to simply cut off the difficult people from your life. Surround yourself with positive people etc. But it is often not that simple. These difficult people can be from all walks of life. They can be acquaintances - easier to walk away from, close friends - a little bit more uncomfortable, because you share the same circle of friends, a partner – a much more painful parting, but the most painful and difficult of all, family. Because there are so many difficult people out in the world and you need to learn to deal with them, here are a few ways to help you deal with difficult people.

Decide if it is worth it

If the difficult person is not causing any catastrophic difficulties, decide if it is worth it to resolve your issues. The difficult person could be with a friend who is being catty and badmouthing you to others, or a partner that is constantly undermining your decisions, a boss that is putting you down. Before confronting a difficult person, it is important to decide whether it is worth it to get past this issue with the other person. You will first have to accept a few things before deciding.

The relation/friendship might end, or that it might move towards a better, healthier relationship. Decide if it is worth your efforts to discuss the problem.

You need to ask yourself if the situation is so bad that it is disrupting your normal life.

Not every issue needs to be argued out; some are minor enough to resolve themselves with time, so you have to decide if the issue is worth the time.

You will have to consider your relationship with the person. Sometimes you will have to accept the behaviour, for example if it is the boss at the workplace, unless it is necessary to resolve, if you need to continue working.

Consider another point; is it a fight you will be able to win? Because if no amount of convincing, fighting or discussion will change their mind, then it is better not to keep trying.

If you have decided that the issue needs to be addressed, then the next step is to arm yourself. Collect all the facts and details of what the issue are the possible solutions etc. You need to for any reaction the other person might have.

Remember that you are not doing this to defeat them but to resolve an issue that you are facing with them. Even if you don't confront them, chances are that they might take the first step and attack you. So be prepared. Learn not to react emotionally.

Use clear and assertive communication

Often these people can take the words you use and twist them to their own purposes, so when you talk to them. Use "I" statements to convey what you are feeling instead of accusing them of something that they may or may not be doing. For example:

"I understand that you were disappointed when I missed dinner with your parents, and I am sorry I couldn't make it. Unfortunately, I had an emergency at work. I will make up for it next time."

Don't say: "You are being unreasonable to think that I would make it in time for the dinner, especially knowing that I called you to say I will not be able to finish work in time for dinner."

Keep the explanations simple

Don't go into details or justify your action. Often the difficult person will not be able to see your point of view and will come to their own conclusion no matter what you say. The more you talk, the higher the chances of conflict are. So when you do talk to them,

Don't be defensive: It is very tempting to try to explain, or defend your actions all the time; it can lead to more arguments and even more issues that will cause conflict instead of solving them. Trying to prove that you are right will only be a waste of energy and time.

Always stay calm

The easiest way to lose control of the situation is by getting emotional. Getting into a fight and having a shouting match will only aggravate the situation. When you are shouting at each other, you have to understand is that no one listening to what the other person is saying.

The only way to resolve an issue successfully is to make sure you can have a calm civilized discussion. The best way you can do this is by calming the other person down enough to actually listen to you.

A person in an emotional state will not listen to reason. If the person is agitated or angry or upset, whatever you say to them is wasted breath. Instead keep your calm, keep your head clear and purposeful with a deep breath.

If the person is crying, allow them to calm themselves down before you approach them to solve the issue. You might know from personal experience that telling a person to stop crying will not stop them from crying.

The ultimate way to make them listen is to sound reasonable and calm, and to not let them agitate you. When you do this, they will slowly come to realize that they are the ones who are acting hysterical and looking bad. They will calm down when they know you won't be provoked.

Talk to a close friend or colleague

If you are having an issue with someone and are not able to move them in any way towards a positive solution then talk to a friend or acquaintance who can act as a mediator. Someone you can trust. Perhaps if the issue is with your mom, maybe your father can help to convince her to come to an understanding.

Maybe it is a fellow student who is causing the trouble and you could look to a mutual friend or a peer to help you mediate and improve the situation.

If you are having issues with a partner, which you are not able to solve by yourselves, go to a relationship counsellor if required.

Limit your interactions

If you are unable to settle the issue no matter what you have tried, the person is not just difficult, but impossible. When such is the case it is best to limit your interactions with the person. Keep the interactions short, to the point and excuse yourself from the presence of the person as soon as possible.

Stay as calm as you can during the conversation, do not react and collect your emotions later on and get over the effect as you know that nothing you do can change the persons behaviour.

Chapter 7: Will Power To Deal With Difficult People

Learn how to master and even enjoy dealing with difficult people

Will Power to Deal with Difficult People

Now that you have a basic knowledge of the different causes and

characteristics that govern difficult people, let us now learn how to

master and, even enjoy, such difficulties.

First things first. If you do not want to deal with difficult people then

you're wasting your time reading this book.

Remember, though, that no place on earth is safe from difficult people.

You really have no choice but to learn how to face them squarely and effectively. Otherwise they will have the power to make you miserable for the rest of your life.

Once there was a person who became fed up with life and so ran away to

the beach and chartered a boat. He went far out onto the ocean and then dived into the deepest part of the Pacific and eventually made his way to the ocean floor.

Surely here he would be able to evade all the difficult people that had

made his life miserable for many years.

While on the ocean floor, he found two tunnels and decided he should

explore them, but wasn't sure which tunnel to take.

He finally went into one of them, but immediately thought to himself:

"Wrong choice! Why did I take this tunnel, I should have taken the

other. I'm an idiot!"

For years he cursed himself for choosing the wrong tunnel, even though

he never left the tunnel he had chosen.

There he was, below the ocean floor, far away from all the difficult

people that had influenced him.

He finally realized that no one else was influencing him. The most

difficult person now affecting him was himself.

There are lessons to be learned from this story:

• You must like people.

Liking people is the first sure step to triumph.

Avoiding people, especially the difficult ones, is a sure road

to becoming difficult yourself.

So go out and meet people. Greet them and genially accept

whatever reaction they give you.

Don't be discouraged but greet more of them regularly until

you get used to them, and until your LOT skyrockets.

Some people may prove to be difficult by being rude but this

doesn't hurt you in any way. It only hurts them.

• Smile.

Most touchy people can be neutralized by a friendly smile.

So practice putting on a pleasant, simple, friendly smile in front of a mirror.

Public speakers and actors study their facial expressions

facing a mirror.

Political and beauty aspirants take time with a photographer

just putting on the best smile that exudes confidence and friendliness.

A smile says it all.

Regardless of how your face looks, a smile always puts on

warmth and comeliness.

A good smile always arrests the temper, even that of difficult

people. So always smile.

- Be sincere.

A smile helps a lot, but sincerity gives your smile credibility.

A mere smile is a matter of facial muscle flexing. When this

alone is involved, the smile becomes unnatural. Put your

heart into it!

A sincere heart will automatically show if you live a life of

sincerity.

Always be sincere in all you do daily.

When your heart gets used to being sincere, smiling sincerely

becomes natural. Difficult people can see right through you, and sincerity melts their hearts.

- Listen well.

Almost every difficult people want to talk much more than

they listen.

This is the main problem in communication. Difficult people

love to talk and want people to listen to them. In a nutshell that's what they are.

Basically, you cannot put two difficult persons together and

have them talk.

Difficult people avoid each other once they recognize each

other.

If they are made to sit down and listen, they won't stand it.

They will either stand up and steal the scene, or just walk out.

If you are with a difficult person, practice becoming a good

listener.

You must learn the wisdom of enjoying listening. Few have

this wisdom.

Most people think there is wisdom in monopolizing a

conversation. As in business, this only results in unfairness and silent protests.

You can make difficult people happy when you just listen to

them.

Not many can do this.

When you are a good listener, even the most difficult people

tend to trust you with their secrets.

Then you begin to know them as they reveal who they really

are. You begin to understand them deeper and will be able to help them better.

• Be agreeable.

This does not necessarily mean agreeing to anything difficult

people say, but it is more about agreeing not to argue.

If you don't agree with the opinions of difficult people, just

listen and send everything to your mental bin.

Delete. It's your right.

Never argue. Never mind if they say you are not

confrontational.

So what?

Nobody dies because of that. But arguments often kill.

Nations go to war because of arguments.

See the wisdom? Remember that every seed of kindness you

plant now will surely reap a harvest of favors soon.

Valuables are often left to agreeable people, never to

aggressive ones. Very few trust contrary people.

If you are known for your politeness, even the most difficult

folks will give you special favors.

Always remember that the most difficult people are strivers.

They are workaholics.

They feed on pressure to hit their goals. Oftentimes they get

promoted to positions that confer favors on "worthy" men.

They often rake in more valuables than the average guy.

- Be honest.

Never flatter anyone insincerely, especially difficult people.

Insincere flattery always traps its users, and it sure is hell to get trapped with a difficult person.

Hence, it always pays to just listen and be agreeable.

When difficult people ask your opinion or ask if you agree

with them, tell them honestly but nicely. If you agree, agree. If you don't, make sure you stress that it is your opinion, not a statement of fact.

Most likely, they will not agree with it and even make you

realize how stupid it is.

Just listen and be polite. Or, if possible and truthful, quote

somebody's opinion that agrees with yours. If they mock it,

at least you save your dignity. Then you can smile more easily.

If you insincerely flatter difficult people and they get to like

you for it, woe to you! You will find it more difficult, and later, impossible to be free from them.

- Praise.

Be certain to take note of their worth and achievements, even

if you think differently and have a different idea for success.

Appreciate their efforts.

Share their triumphs and sad moments.

At times, a smile or tap of congratulations or sympathy is

enough and speaks volumes. But never overdo it.

Practice the steps above daily until you make it your habit.

You will soon possess a healing power that countless people

need and crave. The power that will launch you to untold successes in whatever endeavor you engage in.

If you're not currently doing these 7 Steps as stated above, you need to change your attitude.

Listed below are pointers will help you identify and eliminate bad

attitudes to ensure you are not becoming a difficult person

yourself:

- Respect people always.

Be aware that people, young and old, are entitled to their

rights, beliefs, and opinions.

Without being vocal about it, don't consider yourself to be

better than others.

This will get rid of self-conceit which is the root of disrespect

and being inconsiderate.

Respect authorities in their jurisdictions, whether in the

office, school, malls, public buses, homes, or lands.

Be aware that you cannot impose your own standards and

you have to adjust to their policies.

- Don't compare yourself with others aloud.

You may do so in your mind, but never actually say it.

Different people mostly do things differently and you must

not feel superior with your methods and style.

Likewise, do not compare people with other people verbally.

We have tendencies to compare people, but keep it to yourself.

- Follow a schedule but don't be too rigid with it.

If you are an employer or supervisor, you will surely have

work schedules and deadlines for your employees or subordinates.

But don't be too harsh on the implementation.

Remember that we are only humans - even machines and

computers fail.

People err, get tired or sick, and at times get burned out. They need encouragement.

Give them workloads equal to what you pay them. Be kind to them.

If you are in business, don't get too absorbed in hitting goals

or quotas. There will always be tomorrow, and tomorrow will yield better results.

Learn to let go of things that pressure you. Drop everything

and go out for a while.

Meditate. Look at your surroundings and enjoy them. Smile

at people.

There's more to life than just doing your business or anything

else that keeps you stressed out.

• Enjoy what you are doing, and make sure those working

with you also feel the same way.

Work must support life, and not the other way around.

When work becomes a burden, life merely supports work,

and that will be painful for everyone.

Then, sooner or later, everyone becomes a difficult person.

Every job must become an adventure where every turn makes

you excited to go further.

• Never assume to know everything.

Even if you do, always consider what others have to say,

even if you're a boss.

Accept the fact that there are things you are utterly ignorant

of, no matter how smart you think you are.

If in a meeting among peers you are knowledgeable about a

topic and they are not, it is safer to wait to be asked for your opinion.

It is also good to politely offer your opinion, but do so more

on a note of sharing rather than lecturing.

• Never give unsolicited advice.

Don't give pieces of your "good" advice to people who don't

ask for them, more so to people who don't look like they need them.

Unless you are closely related to such people, or you are

asked for your advice, keep your suggestions to yourself. You may need them more than anyone else does.

• Learn to admit fault and apologize.

It's not important anymore to determine who is right and who is wrong.

When you see that you have hurt a person, whether you are

on the right or wrong side, admit your fault and apologize.

Admitting your fault does not always mean you are wrong. It

may mean you said the right thing at the wrong time in the wrong place. And that's your fault.

It's definitely your fault when you come into a funeral wake

and tell the bereaved that the dead man was a crook and a liar (difficult people can do this).

You may be right, but your rightness will hurt the feelings of

the aggrieved family, and that's your fault.

It's different when the truth needs to be revealed in the name

of justice.

If you have to testify in court that the dead man was a crook

and a liar, though it may hurt the relatives of the deceased, you must say so without hesitation.

- Love must override rules and regulations.

True leaders love their followers and always seek after their

welfare. They do not just put things in order.

Many administrators and managers merely want order and to

see to it that rules and policies are obeyed. This makes many of them difficult people.

Rules and policies are good, but they seldom benefit anybody

except maybe the ones who made them.

Don't decide on matters in a way that negates the personal

choices of other people, like in choosing a lifetime partner, a career, or things to buy.

Guide them but never dictate them.

• Don't be unreasonable.

Make sure your instructions and requirements are within

reach and capacity of other people.

You may be able to do certain things other people can't, and

you have to consider this.

Remember that you yourself also have limited potentials.

• Never humiliate people.

Don't shout at people, or scold them, or curse them,

especially in front of other people.

It's normal to be angry at times when there is a valid reason.

But be careful not to turn anger into hatred.

When anger lasts more than an hour is really potential hatred. Once hatred sets in, a difficult person is born within you; and

you may soon find humiliating another person becomes a normal, or even delightful, activity.

• Nurture a sense of humor.

This is very important. It will keep your sanity intact amid

the fiercest pressure attacks.

Humor keeps your LOT very high, not to mention a healthy

heart and lasting youth. It keeps everything light and easy, even in the worst scenario.

Always find something funny in whatever is happening. As the adage goes, laughter is the best medicine.

A sense of humor can change persons and tight situations.

• Watch your health and diet.

It's hard to control your anger when you're sick, especially

with hypertension or heart ailments.

So eat healthy foods, especially those high in fiber.

Avoid fatty and salty foods, unhealthy drinks, junk foods, and

those high in cholesterol.

Take natural food supplements high in micro-nutrients, and

exercise regularly.

Try to maintain your ideal weight.

Get enough sleep to get ready for tomorrow's new pressures

Your LOT can cope better with pressures if your health

doesn't get in the way.

Chapter 8: Changing Your Environment

Prioritize Your Relationships

Have you ever noticed that the older we get, the busier we become? Each year that passes brings new opportunities, new challenges, and new relationships. It's not like hundreds of people suddenly come into our lives. But each new commitment or relationship adds to the ones we already have until we feel inundated:

Someone recommends a book that's exactly what we were looking for.

We hear about a "must visit" restaurant that's opened.

An old friend connects with us through social media.

New opportunities at church promise personal growth and outreach.

We begin a new relationship that we want to nurture.

A promotion at work provides a bump in pay but greater responsibility.

We're taking classes toward a degree and have to do extensive homework.

Growing kids means growing demands on our time, energy, and sanity.

Notice the common thread: these are all good things. It's not like we're subscribing to the vice-of-the-month club. These are all things we believe can make our life richer, so we want to add them all.

The problem is that we add new activities without getting rid of any old ones. We're not replacing good commitments with better ones; we're simply making a longer list. When we have trouble giving the proper level of attention to each one, we feel guilty.

Marco described his dilemma several weeks ago while attending one of my seminars. He's a seasoned musician, composer, and recording artist, having spent the past fifteen years on concert stages around the world. Now he wants to shift gears and invest in young musicians, using his own experience to mentor them on their career paths.

"I've made a lot of relationships around the world over those years," he said, "and I don't want to give them up. But if I move in this new direction, it's going to take a lot of time and energy. I'll be developing new relationships as this new focus takes off. So how do I build new quality relationships while still maintaining the old ones?"

That's a real dilemma. Most of us face some version of that every day. We add new but we don't want to subtract old. Soon our closets, garages, file cabinets, and even our minds become stuffed to the point that we feel out of control.

To find a good solution, we have to accept one absolute, irrefutable, undeniable fact:

Time is limited. We only have twenty-four hours in a day.

Opportunity Cost

As long as we believe we can do everything and have it all, we'll never solve the problem of being overcommitted. We'll take time management seminars and read self-help books to find ways to cram more into our lives. Those will actually help for a while, but it's like rearranging the deck chairs on the Titanic. It may look better, but it won't keep the ship from going down.

We might think of a person we know who gets more done than us. It's easy to think, "Well, they must have more time than I do." But they have twenty-four hours, just like we have twenty-four hours. Somehow, they're more productive than we are.

However, there's a greater problem. It doesn't matter if we're doing more things if we're not doing the right things.

In economics, the concept is called "opportunity cost." It means that whatever you say yes to, you're automatically saying no to everything else at that time. If you spend an hour in a meeting, you're not exercising, cleaning, or reading during that time. If you're talking to a friend on the phone, you're giving up the opportunity to wash your car. If you take the kids to Disneyland, you're not mowing the lawn.

Those are all good things, but we can only do one thing at a time. Since time is limited, we can't do everything. The only way to survive is to prioritize our choices, deciding which ones would be the best use of our time.

Suppose your house caught on fire and you knew it would be engulfed in flames within minutes. What would you take with you as you ran out the door? Almost everyone gives the same answer: the things that have the most value. The list usually consists of family members, pets, photo albums, and other irreplaceable items. No one rushes back into a burning house to get their favorite mug.

Relationship Cost

The more value something has to us, the more careful we are. That's why we try not to drop our laptop or balance a glass of lemonade on the keyboard.

That principle applies to our relationships as well. We might have a lot of relationships we enjoy, and we value the uniqueness of each connection. But we're limited in the amount of time and energy we have available. When we spend time with one person, we're giving up the opportunity to spend time with someone else. Though it might sound heartless, we need to prioritize our relationships, spending appropriate amounts of time with different people based on their value in our lives.

My wife Diane is more important to me than anyone on the planet. I have a lifelong commitment to her, which means I need to invest most heavily in that relationship. I also have a career and have discovered that certain people tend to think that I should show up. My job is a valuable part of my life and requires a solid chunk of time and commitment. But that takes time away from Diane.

Sometimes I travel, so I'm gone for several days at a time. When that happens, I don't get to spend time with my wife. When I return home, there are many people I could catch up with. But even though those are good relationships, I've learned the value of investing in Diane first. I might change jobs or locations or other situations, but I'm not planning on changing wives.

No Guarantees

Alison goes to the gym four times a week. She joined a spin class and a yoga class. She doesn't eat red meat, grows her own vegetables, and drinks purified water. She takes supplements and wears sunscreen.

Patrick eats bacon four times a week. He watches weight-loss reality shows on television while eating chips. His weight lifting program consists of standing up. He eats mayonnaise from the jar with his fingers. He has installed a soda tap in his garage.

So, who's going to live the longest?

Alison has taken every precaution to protect her health, but she could get hit by a texting driver while walking through a parking lot. Patrick could defy the odds and live to be a hundred.

Is it fair? No. There are no guarantees in life. We plan for the worst but hope for the best. Neither Alison nor Patrick can control every aspect of their lives. Normally, our choices determine our outcomes; but the outcomes are not guaranteed. The only things we have control over are the choices, not the results.

How Long Before My Crazy People Change?

We can only change ourselves. If we think that by hanging in there long enough they'll come around, we'll probably be disappointed. The only way we can avoid being a victim is to make the right choices because those choices are right, not because they might convince someone to change.

It's hard to stay motivated when our crazy person doesn't change. Our willpower runs out, our tank runs dry, and we think, "When will things get better?"

There are no guarantees. It might not get better. They might never change. The only way we can be drama-free in our relationships is to focus on us, not them. We're the ones who can change.

Making healthy choices in our relationships isn't a one-time decision that lasts forever. To stay motivated, we have to keep making those choices day by day, over and over.

Relationships Don't Come with Guarantees

A guarantee is a promise that something will perform as expected. We buy a new car or appliance and we expect it to do what the brochure promised. If that doesn't happen, the manufacturer will either fix it or replace it. Most people won't make a major purchase without that type of guarantee.

Wouldn't it be great if relationships came with guarantees? Any time someone in our lives got crazy, we could call up the store and trade them in for a better model. "I'm sorry," we would say, "this one isn't working. I think we have a lemon. When can I bring him back?"

Life doesn't work that way, however. Like a used car, our relationships come "as is." When something goes wrong, we can try to fix it or work around it. But no matter what we do, the other person might stay broken (which implies that we're not broken). In our society it's common for people to quickly discard relationships when they don't live up to expectations, as evidenced by the high divorce rate. But if we're committed for the long haul, we have to distinguish between the things we can change and the things we can't change.

What can we not change? Other people. What can we change? Ourselves. What do we do when the other person doesn't change? Accept (the reality of the situation) and adapt (change the way we think and respond).

The Bible is filled with passages that describe the need to take responsibility for ourselves rather than others.

"You, then, why do you judge your brother or sister? Or why do you treat them with contempt?" (verse 10)

"Each of us will give an account of ourselves to God." (verse 12)

"Let us stop passing judgment on one another." (verse 13)

The principle is simple: We are only responsible for our own choices and actions. We're not responsible for the choices of others.

So, What's My Job?

If you've had teenagers, you've probably experienced the dilemma. It's our responsibility to guide our kids as they grow into adulthood, and we provide boundaries to steer them in the right direction. The purpose is to help them become responsible adults, being able to function independently and make wise decisions. The older they get, the more the responsibility for those choices transfers from us to them.

Yesterday I went to a park near our house. As I sat by the lake, I watched a family of ducks swimming near the shoreline. The parents swam with one of their ducklings while the second duckling paddled off by itself in a different direction. Soon, several other ducks surrounded the duckling in what appeared to be a threatening way. The duckling began to panic.

The mother left her family and moved toward the group until the other ducks moved away. She then guided her duckling gently back to her family.

Once they were back together, she pecked the little duck so hard he completely submerged in the water. As soon as he came back up, she did it again. He barely broke the surface before it happened a third time.

When to Leave

At forty, Jim has spent his entire career in the banking industry. He knows his way around banking like the back of his hand and could talk about finances in his sleep (and probably does). He's competent in his skills and confident in his abilities.

Over the years, Jim has worked at several different banking institutions. Good situations, bad situations—he's seen it all. But his last job stretched him to the limit.

In his position as director of operations, he had responsibility for a large part of the organization. The bank was struggling, and Jim knew his input could move it back onto solid ground.

The problem was his boss. Usually, bosses are supposed to remove barriers for their employees, freeing them up to use their unique strengths to excel in their work. But this manager was the barrier. He wouldn't listen to Jim's ideas and micromanaged every detail of his position. Jim began to feel devalued and became discouraged and depressed about his situation.

Jim knew he couldn't continue this way long-term. Sure, he could have stormed into his boss's office and yelled, "I can't take it anymore. You're crazy! I quit." But he knew that would be a reactive response and he would regret the consequences of that choice.

First, he tried to change the situation. He used logic, influence, and careful confrontation to change the dynamics of the relationship. He asked businesspeople he respected how they would handle things. He focused on supporting and affirming his superiors. But over time, nothing changed.

Second, he worked on his attitude. Convinced that the situation wouldn't change, Jim realized he could be a victim or a victor. It was easy to be a victim, letting his emotions be controlled by the environment he was in. That's where he began, feeling hopeless and mentally disengaging from his work. But input from caring friends was the catalyst for change. Instead of being a victim, he realized that for now, this was his job. He decided to focus on being dedicated, learning whatever he could from the bad situation while he was still there. He reengaged with his company, giving it his best effort in spite of the people around him. "The turning point," he said, "was when I remembered that I was really working for God, not for these people."

During that time, Jim took the third step: change his environment. He knew it wouldn't be healthy to stay in that situation long-term, so he started looking for a new opportunity. In a tight economy, it seemed like an uphill climb. But with consistent steps, he explored different opportunities while giving 100 percent in his current position. Several months later, he found a new position in a new industry.

The result was the same: he changed jobs. But it wasn't a knee-jerk reaction. He followed a three-step process to ensure the best outcome:

Change the situation

Change your attitude

Change your environment

Jim grew through the process and was able to have a healthy attitude when he left his previous employer.

Our situation may involve different people, but the scenario is the same. Whether it's an unreasonable boss, interfering parents, a demanding spouse, undisciplined kids, nosy neighbors, insensitive friends, or crazy siblings, someone else's choices are creating havoc in our lives.

Sometimes we feel hopeless. We're trapped in a job or a relationship and don't see any way out:

"I'm a single parent, and I can't quit my job."

"My spouse is abusive, but I don't have anywhere to go."

"My sister is driving me crazy, but you can't divorce your sister."

"My parents stick their nose into everything I do, but I can't disrespect them."

"If I confront them or end the relationship, they'll explode—and I don't think I'm ready for that."

These situations all involve people we care about. In fact, that's why they're driving us crazy. Someone we work with could show the same behaviors and we would think it was entertaining. But when it's someone we care about and we feel stuck with them, the situation seems hopeless.

When the tension builds, we wonder how much longer we can put up with it. Everything inside us wants to run away and escape the situation.

So, is leaving a bad thing?

In most cases, it's bad if it's a reactive response. But if it's the last resort of a carefully thought-out process, it could be the healthiest solution.

Should I Leave or Stay?

Since every situation is different, we can't have a one-size-fits-all checklist. That would be handy, but there are as many solutions as there are situations. Generally, all of the solutions fit into one of three actions:

Stay in a bad situation

Leave a bad situation

Stay in a bad situation with a strategy for working on it

Stay in a Bad Situation

Staying in a bad situation with no plan for changing the situation or our response is almost always a bad idea. Ignoring the problems we face won't make them go away. We hope things will get better and that our crazy person will change.

Yes, it's possible—but so is winning the lottery. We know the chances of winning big are almost nonexistent, but we keep buying tickets "just in case."

Why do people stay in bad situations? There could be a number of reasons:

They're afraid of what the crazy person will do if they quit the job or end the relationship.

They're afraid of what will happen to them if they pull out.

They're afraid of what other people will say.

They're afraid of the unknown.

They've always been a victim, so they don't know any other way of living.

They listen to advice from well-meaning friends who are trying to fix them.

They're afraid of conflict.

They're trying to protect the crazy person.

Most of those reasons have to do with fear. That might seem unreasonable, but people have an emotional set point within any situation where the pain is more comfortable than the prospect of the unknown. That's why people often stay in jobs with an abusive boss: it's all they know, whereas taking positive steps is risky.

One of the most dangerous reasons to stay in a bad situation is trying to protect the crazy person. We make excuses for their behavior because we don't want people to think badly of them or because they embarrass us. The problem is that when we protect them, we shield them from the negative consequences of their behavior. If they don't have consequences, they never have an incentive to change. They might apologize and promise things will be different, but promises have to be backed up with performance. Blind loyalty on our part can actually keep healing from happening.

Staying in a bad situation without any plan for change is like constantly putting air in a leaky tire without patching the hole.

Leave a Bad Situation

Leaving should be a calculated choice, making it the last resort after all other options have been exhausted. It might involve quitting a job, changing churches, or moving from a toxic friendship. Leaving too quickly and impulsively rids us of the uncomfortable situation but doesn't resolve the issues that led to the problem in the first place.

Every relationship problem involves interaction between two or more people. The crazy person may be primarily at fault, but we need to consider our contribution as well—how we respond, what we say, the choices we make. If we aren't being realistic by recognizing the reality of our part in the problem, we'll carry those same responses and attitudes into the next situation.

"OK," you say, "I've tried everything possible to change the situation, and it won't budge. They're still crazy. I've worked on my attitude and response, but I'm running out of ammunition. At what point should I consider a change?"

Again, there are no absolutes. But here are the questions to ask yourself:

Am I unable to keep from being a victim?

Do I see myself as less of a person because of the other person's choices?

Am I (or the people I'm responsible for) in danger?

What, exactly, will I be giving up if I leave?

What, exactly, will it cost me to stay?

If I leave, what steps can I take to genuinely resolve these questions?

If you answered yes to any of the first three questions, that doesn't necessarily mean you should make a change. But when added to your answers to the last three questions, it provides the foundation for making a careful decision.

Stay in the Situation, but with a Plan

There's a big difference between staying in a bad situation with no plan and staying with a carefully crafted blueprint. The first is wishful thinking; the second provides genuine hope.

If we make the choice to stay, it shouldn't be because we feel obligated to "hang in there." It should be because we've determined that there is (a) sufficient value in the relationship to make it worth the effort, and (b) sufficient evidence that the other person is willing to participate in the change. If they're not willing to work on it, they won't see any consequences, which means there will be no change. We don't want to impulsively quit a dysfunctional job without something else lined up, but we become victims if we stay without a course of action for improving the situation.

It takes effort to make a blueprint for relationships. It's not quite as hard with casual, irritating relationships. With a spouse or family member, getting help from a professional counselor could be a valuable resource for charting a new course. In any case, the plan needs to design ways of coping with our anger and hurt when it happens, as well as strategies for dealing with painful issues as they arise. We also need a clear delineation of physical and emotional boundaries for the other person. "Good fences make good neighbors," as Robert Frost said. If we're going to stay, we need a plan.

Staying Power

If we decide to stay in a situation, committing energy to make it work, here are suggestions to survive and thrive:

Think through your options. Be sure that the plan is in place before making the decision.

Decide what your nonnegotiables are if you stay—the boundaries that will keep the plan on task.

Find a way to be yourself in the relationship. Pretending that you're OK can drain your energy over time and keep the relationship from growing.

Base everything on truth. Be willing to set aside your fears, prejudices, and inaccurate lenses to see things the way they really are. Look at the facts behind the feelings.

Look at the time you remain in the relationship as a test period where you both work on how you relate to each other. That provides a chance to evaluate evidence of growth or decay. If things fail to progress, go back to the decision-making process about staying or leaving.

It's never healthy to be a martyr. Don't base your identity on the fact that you're hanging in there in a debilitating relationship.

Take ownership of your decision. Recognize that there will be no perfect choice, because every decision has good and bad outcomes. Instead of trying to make exactly the right choice, make a healthy choice and then make it right.

Let the other person take ownership of their side of the relationship. We need to take care of ourselves and let them take care of themselves. Instead of rescuing them, we need to let them make their choices and reap the consequences of those choices.

Committing to a Decision

Write down the names of three people you have the most challenging relationship with and why. Rank them based on their level of challenge. Take the top one and ask: What would be the worst thing that would happen if I left this relationship? What would be the best thing? What would be the worst thing that would happen if I stayed in this relationship? What would be the best thing?

Then show the list to a trusted, objective friend to evaluate if you're seeing clearly or if your own lens is distorted.

There are no easy answers, but looking at our relationships with eyes wide open, we can evaluate and make decisions with wisdom.

Staying in a toxic relationship without a plan is a dangerous choice. Wavering in our decision making isn't healthy either. We might choose to leave, or we might choose to stay. Staying in the middle is a recipe for disaster.

Chapter 9: Gossiping Employees

When Employees Gossip or Complain about the Boss

Who they are: Every manager at one point or another, no matter how well liked or how effective, has either felt the wrath of their team or felt alienated by them from time to time. If you go through your management career with a strong desire to be liked, this can be particularly difficult.

People tend to forget that managers are human too; if you walk into a room and all conversation suspiciously stops, it's not a particularly nice experience. Neither is walking into the pub after work and finding that you are the only person not invited for drinks. As we already know, the phrase 'it's lonely at the top' was invented for a reason.

Ironically, it's sometimes easier to deal with the idea of the team talking about you behind your back when you've given them something to talk about – say redundancies, reprimands, a change in working hours or any other change that they are entitled to share their opinions on.

If you are working hard to be accepted, trusted and liked by the team and find that they are still talking about you and refusing to invite you, however, it can be difficult to take.

Here's my two pence worth on that:

What to do:

First, don't be paranoid. Just because your team are all together and seem a little suspicious, don't get paranoid. They may or may not be talking about you. They could just as easily be talking about the manager in another department that is having an affair with his secretary or the post boy that the women all fancy. Don't be led astray by negative thoughts.

Work with the facts: if you hear them talking about you, you have something to work with. If you don't, you have nothing. Don't go on imagination; you could be wrong and it will be easy to deny anyway.

It's normal! It's going to happen so you have to live with it; it's just one of those things. Workers in every company in every industry across the world get together to whinge about the boss from time to time. It's a unifying theme; in short, it's often how team members bond. I challenge you to find a single employee who hasn't criticised or slagged off the boss in their working life. Indeed, think back to before you moved into the ranks of management; be honest – did you ever do the same? Of course you did. We all did. We just never realised how it felt from the other side before.

Oh by the way: the fact that your team will get together and share their observations about you is just one reason why you need to treat everyone equally, be consistent in your dealings with team members and why you should never pass comment negatively about one employee in front of another. I guarantee you that it will get back to them and will impact on their morale.

Talk to them: Of course, while it is entirely normal that your staff will discuss you when you're not there, you don't want to let it become divisive. Your relationship with your team can be the strongest asset you have; don't let it suffer if you can help it. If you know or suspect that there is a specific reason for the gossiping or complaining – perhaps they are unhappy with a recent decision you made, for instance – talk to them about it. Either meet with team members individually, or talk to the team as a whole, and ask them how they are dealing with the decision you made.

Be prepared to listen to them and confirm you have heard and have taken on-board what they are saying; you can do this by repeating their points back to them to summarise and gain their agreement of the issues in question.

Now you have a choice to make; you can either amend your decision after taking the feedback, or stick with it; I can't help you with that choice. You are going to have the make the decision based on the particular issues at hand.

All I can say is that you shouldn't change or reverse your decision just because staff are vocal about their unhappiness; your role as a manager is to sometimes make the unpopular decisions that are needed to in order for the company to grow. That said a good manager can also be flexible and prepared to admit when they are wrong; if the decision isn't crucial to the success of the company or department and the team bring up issues that you'd never really thought of, don't be afraid to reconsider your decision.

If you do decide to stick with the decision, be prepared to explain your thinking to the team. State why you believe the decision is necessary and run through the consequences of not making the decision. The chances are that once the team feel that they have been listened to, they will be more receptive to your point of view and will understand, if not agree with, the reasons behind the decision. The goal is not to make them change their mind but to be able to move forward as a team together.

A word to the wise here: teams will often be uneasy with major changes that are introduced with little or no consultation. You don't have to ask their permission for every decision you make, but you should try to include them in your thought process or at least explain the reasoning behind your bigger decisions. Thrusting changes on a team with no prior discussion demonstrates lack of respect for your team members. If they have been at the company longer than you, for instance, they may actually know more about certain processes than you do; as such, they are a great resource to use. It's tempting for new managers to want to stamp their authority on a new team and job, but they often do so before they have a full appreciation for the intricacies of the current working process; rather than risk making an unpopular and poorly thought out decision, consult with those workers who can point you in the right direction.

Work harder to bond: If you feel that your team are talking about you behind your back, you may want to try to make yourself more accessible. This may not always help but you'll find that employees often gossip about the boss simply because they don't know you very well and feel little loyalty because they have no access to you as a person. If you see the team in the pub after work, for instance, why not ask if you can join them? Show them your human side; spend some time with them outside of the work environment. Buying a round of drinks always helps to foster good feeling!

If you are struggling to bond with your team, invite them to a department-sponsored bonding event. You could opt for a formal team building or team bonding session with outside experts or simply throw some money in the kitty and take them to the pub, for a meal, bowling or even playing rounders in the park on a sunny day, with beer and burgers thrown in afterwards. Whatever you do, make it fun so it doesn't feel like work. Once the team can relate to you as a person as well as the boss, things tend to get a little easier.

Assuming you want to talk to your employees about an unpopular decision you recently made, let's imagine how that discussion with your team could go:

Manager: "Hi everyone; thanks for coming. I've called you all here today because I want us to talk about how things are going. I made some pretty big changes last week and I want to see how they are impacting on you. Does anyone want to tell me how they're getting on after the changes?"

Employee one: "I will. I'm not happy with them."

Manager: "OK, can you tell me why?"

Employee one: "It means more work for me; I have to take on more responsibilities without any more money and without any recognition."

Employee two: "I think it was wrong to let Julie and Emma go like that; they were nice women. We could have worked something out."

Employee three: "Yes, they were our friends and now we have to take on their work."

Employee four: "It does make you wonder who is next."

Employee one: "Yes it does. And another thing – the procedures you've got us using now don't make sense at all. I now have to speak to three people instead of one and get them all to sign off on the purchase order before I can do anything."

Manager: "Any other concerns?"

All: Silence.

Manager: "Thanks for telling me honestly how you feel, I appreciate that and I have been listening to you. As I see it, you are upset that friends of yours lost their jobs and that you have had to take on their work. Jackie, you are also frustrated about what you perceive as a convoluted accounting procedure, is that right? Have I summarised the problems accurately?"

All: Nods.

Manager: "OK, well let me take the time to discuss my thoughts with you. I obviously can't go into detail about Julie and Emma's situations, other than to say that the decisions we took were purely about the work roles and not the people. I agree with you that Julie and Emma are nice women. However, as I hope you appreciate, it would be inappropriate of me to talk in detail about either of them with the rest of the team.

"What I can say is that we're in a tough economy right now and we have to make some tough decisions. We spent a lot of time assessing the situation and the plain fact of the matter was that a significant proportion of the work Emma and Julie were doing was already being duplicated elsewhere, some in our own department and some across the company.

"As businessmen and women, we have to look at the bottom line; we owe it to the company, our customers and to our workforce to be as efficient as possible. The decisions we made and I instigated were related to that.

"I understand that it has passed a little bit more work onto some of you; I don't believe any one person is taking on those jobs wholesale, however, because there is no need for that. What work wasn't already being duplicated has been spread around the rest of the team. I'm very happy for us to discuss exactly what work is now being done by whom to make sure no-one is taking on more than they need to, but again, I say that we are in a tough economy and we must all pull together for the good of the company.

"Now Jackie, I can understand your frustration regarding needing three people from across the company to sign off on new purchases. On the face of it, it does sound inefficient.

"I can tell you that we instigated that procedure to stop waste after we discovered that different departments were spending a considerable amount of money buying in the same products. There was no communication between us and money was simply being flushed down the pan. That said, you are right to bring it up.

"I'd love to talk to you to get your ideas on how we can effectively streamline the situation without incurring the same problems as before. Can we get together next week to discuss it?"

Conclusion

I can remember one day in particular when I had been so annoyed by someone that I felt completely out of character. Why was I allowing this person to annoy me to the point that made me feel so full of rage? How did this person have the power to affect me in this way? I had to take a deep breath and then I decided to do A LOT OF RESEARCH! After my research, I came to the following conclusion: If someone could infuriate and affect me this severely, then there was something that I needed to work on. I needed to point the finger at myself. How could I allow others to alter my positive disposition just because they are used to being difficult? It became crystal clear to me that difficult people are who they are and that I do not need to succumb to their despair; therefore I should never allow others to alter my mood.

I cannot control others, but I CAN however, control how I feel. I had to ask myself: Why should I allow someone else destroy my beautiful day because they may be miserable? Even times when I was experiencing momentary chaos in my personal life, I never took my issue out on others because that's not right. Realizing this is why difficult people have changed my life forever! Now, instead of allowing someone to approach me with their irrational intentions, I am always ready to radiate my sunshine and there is NO STOPPING MY LIGHT!

Don't let anyone cover your sunshine ever! Your sunshine is your happiness! Just keep pushing forward with your personal development and hopefully others will be inspired by your outlook along the way. Also, I urge you to read as much as you can on this topic so that you can get a sense of empowerment in this area. I believe that no one resource has all of the answers, so always research as much as you can. Also, you can never know enough, so there is always room for improvement.

I hope this book was able to help you to be familiar with the four main types of difficult people and how to deal with each one of them effectively. I also hope that you have learned something valuable about your sunshine. The next step is to apply all you have learned and are comfortable with into your day to day interaction and make a commitment to improve your relationships with other people, including those that are challenging and difficult.

Thank you again for downloading this book!

www.ingramcontent.com/pod-product-compliance
Lightning Source LLC
LaVergne TN
LVHW010355020525
810227LV00021B/402